CW01660815

HOW TO EXIT A BURNING BUILDING

Edited by Christina Thatcher

Foreword by Mark Blayney

Judge's Report by Rachel Trezise

PARTHIAN

Parthian, Cardigan SA43 1ED
www.parthianbooks.com
First published in 2015

ISBN 978-1-910901-05-2
Edited by Christina Thatcher
Cover artist: Pria Borg-Marks
Cover designer: Simon L. Read
Typeset by Elaine Sharples
Printed in EU by Pulsio SARL
Published with the financial support of the Welsh Books Council
British Library Cataloguing in Publication Data
A cataloguing record for this book is available from the British Library.

CONTENTS

INTRODUCTION

The Welsh Writers' Trust was formed in 1986 to support and encourage English writing in Wales. In this time the Trust has helped nurture both new and well-established creative writing talent and has helped many of the current stalwarts of the Wales literary scene on their way to success.

Part of the Trust's aim is to provide a platform for new voices – to give access for talented and inspiring writers and help launch their careers. The Robin Reeves Prize for Young Writers Competition was established for this very reason. Editor of *New Welsh Review* for a decade, Robin was a passionate advocate of developing Wales' identity both culturally and politically, and helped build the foundations for the post-devolution landscape that we now take for granted. Robin was also a founder member and Chairman of the Trust.

This is the second time the competition has been held in Robin's memory. Young writers between the ages of 17–24 were invited to submit on the theme of 'Out of the Ashes – Overcoming Adversity'. Within this field, writers could explore the subject of moving beyond trauma, difficulty or hardship in any way they wanted to; personal, political or cultural.

The remit was much broader than competitions of this type often are. Writers were encouraged to submit the fullest imaginative range possible: poetry, fiction, drama or creative non-fiction, in either complete works or as excerpts. The results were, as we'd hoped, rich in their interpretations of the theme and wide-ranging in scope. This made the task of judging all the harder, and so we were thrilled to have Dylan Thomas Prize-winning author Rachel Trezise on board to make the tough decision of choosing an eventual winner.

As well as seeing her work in print, the winner of the Prize – Natalie Ann Holborow – receives £500 for her remarkable story 'The Bees'. There are also prizes of £100 and £50 for the two runners-up, Eve Elizabeth Moriarty and Mari Ellis Dunning, and the other pieces in this collection were shortlisted from the entries received.

The Trust is also delighted to be working with Parthian Books to publish this anthology and bring the young authors highlighted here to a wider audience. Parthian have shown an unstinting commitment to the Wales literary scene over the past twenty-two years and I hope the relationship with the Trust is one that will continue to mature and blossom.

With its thirtieth anniversary just round the corner, the Welsh Writers' Trust is currently at a crossroads as we look to develop the Trust and decide how best we can support and engage with creative writers over the next thirty years. I'm excited to be involved at this time of regeneration and hope that the Trust can continue its work to help the writers we have today and promote the writers of tomorrow.

Mark Blayney, Trustee, Welsh Writers' Trust

ACKNOWLEDGEMENTS

The Welsh Writers' Trust would like to extend our thanks to Richards Thomas Solicitors whose generous sponsorship made our second Robin Reeves Prize for Young Writers Competition, as well as the publication of this anthology, possible.

We would also like to thank our interns, Rebecca Roy, Jodie Kay Ashdown and Renn Hubbuck, for their help in promoting and marketing the competition.

The Trust is also grateful to Pria Borg-Marks for supplying the artwork for our cover as well as to Simon L. Read for the time and creativity he invested in the design.

Finally, we would like to thank everyone who submitted work for the competition. We greatly enjoyed reading each piece which made the selection process for the anthology particularly difficult.

All entry fees, donations and sales of this anthology will be used to fund future competitions or provide financial support for Welsh writers.

JUDGE'S CHOICE: FIRST PRIZE

Natalie Ann Holborow

The Bees

Have you ever watched a bee staggering across the kitchen tiles and, forgetting the fat stinger hidden under its fuzzy brown arse, not felt sorry for it as it hums and crawls to the grave? I watched it go, tracking the sticky linoleum of Mam's kitchen where the floor was still a slippery sheen from bleaching the cat's pee this morning.

When I die, I hope I am not sliding along on my belly through citrus bleach and piss.

Emmy squatted in her summer dress and reached out her hand.

'No, Emmy,' I warned, pulling her little arm back. 'Bees have stingers.'

Emmy's brow puckered into a frown. 'It needs to fly,' she said.

'No it doesn't. It needs to be alone now.'

'Why?'

'It's trying to sleep.'

'Is it going to die?'

I said nothing.

'If I don't help it, then how is it going to fly to heaven?'

I sighed and tapped the edge of her plate with my spoon. Gold butter puddled the toast, the bread clammy and pale.

Mam didn't have a lot of patience with the grill. 'Come and eat your breakfast Em, before it goes cold.' I tapped the plate again. 'You like dippy eggs.'

She sat back down in her chair without taking her eyes off the little bee. It buzzed furiously, staggered on one side and fell still again. If it could buzz out a full sentence, it would tell me *'Christ, this dying thing is knackering.'* Emmy pierced her bubble of yolk with her spoon, liquid gold bursting on stainless steel.

'Duw duw, I don't know, I told 'im see, I *told* 'im he was gonna end up hurtin' himself and what does he bloody go and do?' Mam thundered into the kitchen in her lavender slippers and rose-coloured cardigan, hair scraped tight at the back of her neck. She glanced at us both from behind the armful of dirty bedsheets hugged against her breasts.

'It bloody *'urt*!' Big cousin Jonty burst in, sucking his finger, eyes watery but he wasn't crying, just in pain. Jonty didn't cry. I don't think Jonty was even able to cry. He stopped and stared at his finger in the dirty light falling through the net curtain, the joint plum-purple and shining with spit.

'Well I told you, mun, I said—'

'Yeah well it's no good now, isit? I gots an injury now, look at it, it's gone *'uge* and you don' even care—'

'Oh, for Christ's sake,' Mam snapped, slamming the basket of washing onto the worktop. A cat scuttled out from behind it and disappeared into the lounge. She grabbed Jonty's hand. 'Gis' a look then.'

'Ow,' Jonty moaned, writhing in Mam's bear-grip. 'You's makin' it worse!'

'Oh you'll be fine, man up.' She dropped his hand and daubed at the drops of sweat pearling over her cheeks. 'Bloody boiling in 'ere and you kids are stressin' me out.'

She pushed aside the net curtain and opened the window. A low hum rose from the pots of Bizzy Lizzies below. 'Next door and them sodding bees... they're everywhere. Who the 'ell keeps bees for pets? As if that noisy little rat of a dog weren't enough, they gots to go and get bloody *bees*... they'll be in 'ere again now floating in my bloody coffee...'

'If we didn't have bees, we'd die,' I told her. 'Our Biology teacher said.'

'Bollocks to ew Biology teacher, I don' want no bees on my breakfast.' A can of insect-killing spray gleamed on the windowsill. 'They costin' me a fortune in bee-killer.' She frowned at Jonty. 'And plasters.'

She took a step back. The struggling bee crushed under her slipper.

*

'I gots an idea,' said Jonty, his grazed and freckled legs swinging up over the fence at the bottom of the garden. He grinned at us through the blackberry bushes and stinging nettles. I checked the ground for glass before pulling myself up after him. Jonty's finger was wrapped up in a frog plaster.

'What idea?' asked Emmy, her summer dress tucking up into her knickers as she clambered. We'd made it through the overgrown bottom half of the garden, sliding over broken pots and three-legged patio chairs. Planks of timber sticking up from the weeds like broken fingers.

'Yeah, what big idea?' I nodded at Jonty's injury. 'You're full of big ideas today.'

'Piss off,' Jonty said and Emmy gasped. He fixed his icy little eyes on me. 'You rather go an' help ew Mam with the ironing, issit? Shut up then.'

I frowned at him and followed him through the bushes. Emmy went between us, her copper pigtails bobbing above the brambles.

'Where are we going?' I asked, squinting up through the sunlight. I could smell grass and dogshit. A car roared past on the road behind, bare arms of topless boys dangling and waving from the open windows as a pulse of music drummed out and faded along with the engine. I imagined one day Jonty would do things like that too.

'Payin' next door a visit.'

'Why?'

'You'll see.' Jonty had a can of cheap deodorant sticking out of his arse pocket.

'Are we going to kick the dog?' asked Emmy.

'No.'

'I don't like that dog. It barks at me when I go and smooth it.'

'That's cos it's a little shit.' Jonty glanced back at her. 'Feel free to kick it if you want though.'

'Jonty,' I hissed. Emmy was only six.

We broke into their garden through a little gap in the fence Jonty had made last summer with a clumpy pair of Nikes and a strong kick. Emmy popped her head up, looking back at Mam's shape pegging out the washing, shooing the cat with a slippered foot. 'What if Mammy sees us?'

'What's she gonna do if she does?' scoffed Jonty, rolling himself out into the weeds. 'She's not gonna fit through the bloody fence after us, is she?'

Crouched low on our knees, ducking and slipping behind the clusters of Japanese knotweed and crab-apple trees, we could already hear them. Thousands of them. Have you ever heard the sound of a thousand bees? Swarms of fat yellow bees, rising and dancing in slow circles, backsides bobbing and deadly. The sound of one bee was a warning, a mild irritation— at best an echo of summertime picnics in the park with guarded mouthfuls of jam sandwiches.

A thousand bees was something quite different.

'Jonty what are you doing?' I hissed as he dived behind the shed and smirked at the beehive. The drones rose like dust-clouds. 'You've already been stung once and made a big deal out of it, why would you want to—'

'Shush, mun.' Jonty pressed his plastered finger against his lips. His mouth was a carving in a pumpkin, a sinister grin, as though someone had taken a kitchen knife and sliced it into his face then dropped a lit candle behind his eyes. And then there was the orangey hair, sticking upwards like an awkward stalk.

Revenge. I watched as he slithered out from behind the shed on his belly and into a patch of white borage-flowers, stiff white constellations springing out from the earth. Starflowers, Mam had said once, picking up a white flowerhead that had somehow sailed into our garden. Emmy had been fascinated and thought the sky was falling.

Jonty's hand wrapped around the aerosol can. Of course he wanted revenge.

'These fuckers won't be stickin' no stingers in no one again,' he said, deodorant can in one hand and with the other he fished out a disposable green lighter from his jeans pocket.

'Jonty, don't be stupid,' I hissed, crawling after him. I stuck my hand out to stop Emmy from following. 'You'll get attacked by a thousand of them!'

'They won't be attackin' nothin' when they's on fire.' He released a puff of spray from the can. It drifted back on the breeze, reeking of the classroom when the boys had poured in, sweaty and drenched in spray after PE.

Jonty's eyes flickered. A little flame leapt from his fist. 'Get behind the shed girls and get ready to fuckin' *run.*'

The deodorant can screamed and exploded. In that moment, as if time itself had hovered and hummed, all we saw was black and yellow— the fire and the smoke.

The honey and the bees.

JUDGE'S CHOICE: SECOND PRIZE

Eve Elizabeth Moriarty

Caer Alyn

We delivered without gloves,
scab-kneed and red-handed
in the slick wetness of *Caer Alyn* clay.
The pot-head crowning: a little past
born again, a terracotta nothing
cradled in trowel-tired arms.

The brow of earth mopped clean of dirt,
we pushed on, cutting the next trench
carefully, sorting past shards of plates,
the spines of mice, fingers twisting
in the belly of the ground. Desperate
for signs of life – finger bones,
babies' teeth, slips of skull.

The women who lived here must
have done this too: coaxed life
from one another in turn. Now we
pull them towards us in pieces,
each scrap a something, building
them back from the dead –
appearing in our trays, each day:

a woman, a woman, a child.

JUDGE'S CHOICE: THIRD PRIZE

Mari Ellis Dunning

Fy'n Iaeth

I tuk my first steps in Ponty,
tiny DM's clunkin' an' stompin',
trippin' over shoelaces
like my tongue had tripped over
the alphabet days before.

My first word was a Welsh one –
'dwr', I bin told, an' Mam always
says I 'aven' shurrup since.

She says, 'you've got an MA,
why are you talking like that?'
So I scrunch my hands and pierce
my tongue, pink betrayer, muffling
my 'byears' and 'bithers.'

She says irs not tidy to say 'tidy',
bur I carn stop pronouncing 'ear',
'here,' and 'year,' all the same,
even if it dun sound 'posh'.

I'm in between, speaking a few
languages, feelin' academia

on the tips of my fingers
while my accent sits like fur
on my teeth.

Bur the thing is, tha' first word
led me to Aberystwyth,
to live by the Welsh sea, feeling
it's comforting salt spray –
I must have always liked '*dwr*'.

An' the thing is, people always
know where I'm from,
so I should know it too,
an' I do. I'm from down south.

When I write, I do it right,
bur I speak how I want,
in my own mixture of *iaethoedd*.

Dwi'n siarad Cymraeg,
an' I speak English,
an' sometimes, I gerrem
all muddled up an' say thins like
'I'm proud *o fle dwi'n dod*'.

Appendix

'Fy'n Iaeth' .... My Language
'Dwr' .... Water
'Iaethoedd' .... Languages
'Dwi'n siarad Cymraeg' .... I speak Welsh
'O fle dwi'n dod' .... Of where I come from

COMMENDED

Paige Smeaton

The Day of the Flood

Not so far from Dre-Hen is a drowned little seagull-dead town called Porth. Here there are more pubs than the whole of London; they cabaret wetly through the damp bog sea spray. Inside lurk murders of *beibl* carrying farmers huddled in dark corners *siarad-ing Cymraeg* until the cows come home. This is where I grew up –

But this is irrelevant.

Dre-Hen is a well thrown stone's throw down the coast: the journey takes fifteen minutes by car. This is a place where people live. Let's put it like this:

Lingerie dries salty in the sea breeze. Dre-Hen's wind-rattled chimney tops smoke like old industrial lungs keeping the winter out.

One by one Howell Jones stacks his books watching winter beat the glass and clatter the trees. First by genre then by name. The ones he loves best are furthest out of reach. He imagines living in the old world: his thoughts oscillate like dreams, vibrating through his guts lungs heart teeth. They play like this:

He ripped them out and repackaged them neatly. He caressed her breasts in a second. His fingers strayed over the nipple and it became flat and feathered. Her thighs her buttocks her hair were pulled down in his hands and thrown into the air. He consumed her body and spat it out and –

When she opened her eyes she was an owl.

Howell grabs a pencil and notes it down.

Closer to the harbour Maria Carter collects her laundry before the rain collects it for her. It is too late; her clothes are already damp with the spit of the sea. Howell was right; a storm is brewing in the teapot bay.

On the crest of the hill Oscar Penniman plays his piano alone in the hall. The middle-C echoes off-key through the empty building. The weather warns of a storm, Mrs Evans is watching the bulletin down the hill and in the chest of Dre-Hen. Young Tommy Evans plays chess in front of the screen.

'You can't play chess on your own,' his mother says. He does not listen; Dan de Wolf makes his move.

Howell has just come back from the greengrocer on Chalybeate Street. He has fresh mangoes; he leaves them on the wooden shop floor as he locks away the books and retires to bed. Next door to the Evans', Maria Carter folds her laundry in front of the cracking furnace.

Everywhere, everyone is retiring to bed as the sea begins to boil.

The sun crawls hungover over the hills as Old Mrs Peterson wades through a town submerged. Her chest is full of Dunkirk spirit; the water whets her appetite.

Today the sea holds Dre-Hen in its hands: it shakes and rattles the toy town, squeezing them all between its thumbs. Windows, eyes, doors open to discover a world now beach-kissed, stone-kicked, salt-lipped, wind-whipped, shell-cut, sand-spat, sea-flat. Later a thousand umbrellas and waders will blossom through the debris; now only Old Mrs Peterson braves the calm. She commands the water like a steam cruiser as she searches for a harbour large enough to dock.

Around her people begin to emerge but the sea wrings

them out and sends them back. Old Mrs Peterson sails on; she is a woman on a mission:

'Loo roll, toothpaste, mangoes.'

Her sharp eyes peruse the shops as she cruises down the street. On her way she passes Dre-Hen Books –

Howell has dropped the key and now it flows downstream over the cobbles and down the streets. Howell's mouth is a perfect 'O' like a yawning cat's (but he is not relaxed), it melts into a grimace as his books begin to float. The water trickles in and browses titles with wet fingers. Helpless, Howell watches as his shop falls 20,000 leagues under the sea.

Up town Oscar pauses at Dre-Hen's new shore. He had seen the beginnings of the storm on the news last night: the waves crashed five storeys high, what a story! Behind him fifty resolute sandbags are stacked packed against the windows of Dre-Hen's discount supermarket. Ahead he imagines the music shop bobbing like a boat lost in a winter ocean.

As Oscar turns back Maria strides forward. Wielding her bin-bag-lined trolley she assaults the water in her waders. They are bright yellow and she cuts through the sea like sunlight. At home her husband Simon sits in the loft; he wraps himself in neurotic fear and quilts. Around his waist he has pulled the cord of his nightgown tight: he sits in darkness, there is no light.

Meanwhile downstream Dan de Wolf finds a silver key. Young Tommy Evans takes it. They pretend it is a pirate's key, a key to hidden treasure. Together they run through, up, down and out the town's muddy canals.

Together they rush past Old Mrs Peterson. Her wake knocks them off kilter; Dan de Wolf makes her out as the pirate ship:

'Ahoy!'

Reaching her harbour Old Mrs Peterson knocks with a wry spry rap-a-tat of the wrist on the grocer's cabbage-green door. Old Mrs Peterson asks after fresh mangoes: they are all out.

On the crumbling promenade umbrellas unite against the grey sea spray and marvel over crushed marble and smashed granite. They heave in unison like the waves as they sweep up and down and up and down the prom. A thousand wellingtons erode down the remaining rock, wall, crunch the sand and kick the stones. Maria picks up a lump of marble and places it in her trolley as a souvenir. A lump of rock from the seaside, she imagines Dre-Hen's name at its core.

At Dre-Hen Books the sea is considering Orwell. It licks the base of the spine as Howell watches in distress; it is like a bad seduction. As the waves consume the pages the marriage is consummated. Howell bangs on the glass, he has no spare key. His own is unlocking pirate treasure down town. On the good ship *Jolly Roger* Young Tommy Evans and Dan de Wolf resist a stormtossed sea. 'A Heave Ho me hearties!' they cry without knowing what it means. Turning starboard they sail up the Main Street splashing havoc as they go.

The umbrellas evaporate down streets and into houses as the national news arrives to salvage the wreckage of a story. Spotting Old Mrs Peterson they approach her as she steams over and through the rubble – but Old Mrs Peterson just wants to talk about:

'Mangoes, I can't find any anywhere, what has the world come to?'

They push the storm.

'That's no excuse, even in the war we had fruit.' They edit her out of the footage.

Taking their cameras through Dre-Hen they discover Howell; he is introduced to the audience as a desolate business man. They ask him his opinion on global warming.

'It's beautiful,' he says.

The presenter is taken aback: 'What?'

'*Nineteen Eighty-Four*,' sighs Howell, 'it floats.'

Young Tommy Evans spills into the house drenched from pirate hat to pirate boot. Mrs Evans is not pleased; she punishes him with cold soup and he is sent to bed. Worst of all she confiscates the key. It is thrown out as a piece of rubbish. Tommy sulks and resolves to give her none of his imagined loot.

Elsewhere a rival news crew stop Oscar on his way home. They ask him where he lives.

'On a hill,' is his reply.

The cameras vanish, pulled out to sea once more.

Dre-Hen seeps through the nation leaking into television screens and radio sets. It is too late now: the sea has drawn back leaving viewers marooned. Mrs Evans is watching the bulletin when Old Mrs Peterson knocks on her front door.

'Excuse me dear, do you have any toothpaste?'

Upstairs Young Tommy is hungry. Dan de Wolf offers a biscuit.

'How about mangoes?'

The adults' voices soak through the ceiling. Old Mrs Peterson turns away disappointed.

Sailing down the Main Street she sees Howell with Maria Carter. Maria has given him a cup of hot chocolate bought from a brave café. Old Mrs Peterson enquires as to fresh mangoes.

'I had mangoes,' was his sad reply, 'I've lost my key; I can't get in to let the water out—'

The steamboat of a woman takes his hand and throws Howell a lifeline. It bobs like a buoy on her tongue:

'Would you like to sleep on my sofa tonight?'

Nodding, Howell is taken under the dark sails of Old Mrs Peterson as Maria Carter pushes her trolley home.

The sea lounged in the bed of the bay as the hours killed the day of those who live in Dre-Hen. Above it all the sun drinks away into the night as:

Young Tommy Evans shivers in a bed sailing the seven seas; *Nineteen Eighty-Four* sinks; Maria Carter holds her husband in his dread; the news reels rattle down and Old Mrs Peterson settles for oranges.

And in the morning the sun will crawl hungover but triumphant over the hills again.

Ellen Davies

Relocation

They say we should leave the Valleys,
seek out new life in the city
where our minds, not our hands
can pay the way, where there is opportunity
for everyone, even the men
who haven't worked a day
since the pit wheel ceased spinning,
the iron smelting, where there is not
a church, pub, shop shut on every corner
and children are promised more
than their place in the queue for dole.
But I turn to these peaks, washed green,
their paths cleared of coal rubble;
we've sunk lakes where shafts sent men
into the black, and trees heal
the slag heap scars of our *cwm*.
How can we abandon this
for somewhere they tell us will be better?
So we stay,
resolved to remain disadvantaged.

Eve Elizabeth Moriarty

wolf-girl

that winter, you starved yourself hairy,
thick fur clouding arms, legs,
clinging like fat to a bone:
wolf-girl, growling in hunger,
biting your own tail against the cold.

waxing away hours in your room,
ripping thick red rectangles into flesh –
the coat coming back days later,
bone-body trying to smother its shivering.

the moon, full and full again without blood,
lunatic, sharpening your teeth on cubes of ice
alone, whimpering in dens of blankets,
shrinking yourself back to a cub.

the pack of housemates out for dinner
and you, alone, your cave-stomach howling
at the sky.

Niall Robert Ivin

The Bank

She spoke to the pretty young man and explained. The tele got pawned three weeks ago. Her last meal was two days ago. Half a tin of beans on bread five days gone. Woodlice were looking savoury. She held back that last detail but her hands trembled on the pseudo-pine counter and tried to betray her. He considered her through the little holes in the glass and smiled. The glass wasn't the only thing that separated them. They appeared two distinct species.

'We may be able to help you out, I'll see what's available,' he said.

He looked down and started typing, staring at the monitor and clicking furiously. It seemed a secret language to her, clean and precise like his appearance. He stood and gave her a quick nod and slinked through a door behind him. She looked at the thin, tough glass that separated them and saw the loudness behind her in the reflection. It was all sorts of people, desperate like her. Shabby like her. This was her first time at the bank and she wondered if the regulars minded new people. Her hands began to tremble again so she lowered them and willed them to comfort each other but it felt unnatural. A forced marriage. The pretty young man returned and she condensed back into reality.

'We do have an offer that might be suitable,' he said smiling, again. 'It should see you through a fortnight, maybe a month if you're prudent.'

She nodded. He reciprocated, avoiding proper eye contact. He couldn't bear to see her soul. He looked at her drawn cheeks and her bony chin instead and wondered what had messed it all up for her.

'There are a couple of things that need to be settled before we can finalise the loan,' he said.

Her lips drew tight, like overstretched elastic bands. She was one big bundle of them these days, bouncing around waiting to unravel or start snapping. When elastic bands snap it's always sudden and people are always surprised. Dark trenches set in about her face, about her lips, under her eyes and her forehead. They deepened themselves in frenzy and then waited.

'What we need is something to secure the loan. If you don't have something on you now to secure it we can hold the package for two hours, but then we'll have to void the request.'

The impact left her face deadpan; the trenches had caved in on themselves or been blasted out. She had known it was coming. That was why she brought it. Better it went here than down the cash converters. She wouldn't have to see magpies picking over it when she walked down the high street. It would be gone and that would be the end of it.

She unclasped the chain and presented it to the pretty young man.

'That should do nicely,' he said when he felt the weight of it. He savoured it in his hand, raising and lowering it. She waited to see if he'd give it a nibble like they did in the films but he didn't. He slipped it into an envelope and slid a piece of paper and a pen under the glass to her. She put her mark on the page. Behind her the door to the bank started closing and opening itself, chiming every few seconds. The queue was out the door and the sensor didn't understand. Welcome to my life, she thought.

The pretty young man stood again and gestured to his left. She moved across to a small metal shutter near her shins. The young man picked up a phone and finalised the withdrawal. She couldn't hear what he said, there weren't any holes in the glass now. The smoke of overworked engines seeped into the lobby through the frantic doorway. The sound of their rattling whine mingled with the rattling whines of the desperate mass behind her. Through a big metal door behind the glass came a new man who was older and far less pretty. He leaned forward and dropped the cardboard box. She heard it hit the shutter. So did the reflected mass. Their faces jerked toward her in unison and it made her spine feel funny. The pretty young man pressed a button and smiled and then the shutter opened. It hit her shins hard, but she didn't react to it and mechanically picked up the box.

When she raised herself the young man was already serving a new customer, nodding and smiling and looking at her chin. She walked past the grey, coughing mass to the fraught doorway and timed her exit so they didn't shut on her. The streets were wet and quiet. She put the box down on the cracked pavement and peeled open the flaps. She saw the tins and the sachets huddled together and couldn't help but feel a prick of hope.

They may yet, be okay.

Natalie Thomas

A Lid on my Fears

Seven thirty am. A Wednesday morning
like any other:
hot cup of tea, towel-dried hair, woolly coat
and out into the daylight –
that morning light that feels somehow hollow, cold
as if waiting for the heaviness of the afternoon.
I arrive early, twenty minutes filling out forms,
tapping anxious toes.
She calls my name the way doctors do –
the way you never do –
distant, with a rising tone,
like my name is somehow a question.
She takes me into her office
and sinks into the curves of her seat,
as if curling into the familiar contours of a lover.
I balance on the edge of a chair.
Her eyes read my body, my rigidity,
don't worry this is all confidential she says.
So we speak. *Confidentially.*
Not the way I speak to you about my secrets,
two people avoiding the day by sharing hopes and regrets,
you kneading my tense shoulders and me drawing circles
with my fingers around your bellybutton.
No, in here secrets are not poetry, they are mathematics.

The light becomes dense, thick with the weight
of the hours passed. Hot on bare shoulders as I sit, stare.
You ring me. Don't ask if I'm alright but tell me you are proud
as though you don't think there is anything wrong with me.
In your eyes, I am the same, untarnished me.
I am more than my problem.
I am the swells and valleys of my body,
the soft hum of my voice
in the early morning, the freckled, milky skin
beneath your fingers.
I am a known landscape. Home.
I tell you about my day, about treatment.
You reply that we can get through it together.
We'll put jam on our faces and see how long
we can last without washing it off.
Like that game we used to play at school
when we got doughnuts from the local Co-op
and tried not to lick our sticky, sugar dusted lips.
A minor victory for someone who hates dirt.
Grease.
Contamination.
I want to ask if you love me less. But I know that you don't.
You turn something terrifying into something sweet,
fruity and delicious. You put a gingham lid on my fears,
and make sure that they don't spill out and catch me.

Natalie Thomas

Pso-ri-a-sis

There are times when I feel at one
with my body and there are other times when I don't.
Sometimes, when we lie in bed, stripped, vulnerable
I place his hand on the swell of my hip,
let him touch what makes me *me*.
It makes me feel like a woman.
Sometimes, before I get in the shower, I look at my reflection,
at the places he loves most. My breasts,
small, freckled and perfectly moulded to the dish of his hands.
My back, lined by my long, thin spine
like the dark seams on the reverse of 1950s stockings.
Sometimes, I don't look.
I ignore the blemishes that make me *me* –
the blemishes that make me feel
disconnected. Separate from my body.
That make me hide it away
and forget
that I am more than words and thoughts.
Forget that I am a form too.
Sometimes I write it on medical documents, *psoriasis* –
a tricky word to spell. Silent 'p's always creep up on you
like raw, red patches of skin on your knees and elbows.

Sometimes, when we lie in bed, stripped, vulnerable,
I let him trace my legs with his hands,
let him kiss each patch of imperfect skin,
it makes me whole.

Sam Pryce

The Concealed

They take one look at me and something in their faces alters. Believe me, I see it every day. Granted, it is more obvious in some than in others. So much so that I have become accustomed to the shudders, the glowering; the wide and dead eyes; the tight lips and flared nostrils. They veil their contempt with averted gazes, dipped eyelids.

I am walking down the cobbled main street of this idle town – one I cannot call home. The familiar bruised sky hangs above, its stubborn clouds muffling the sun. My bags, full and sentenced to life, dig into my hands. I am not unlike the others, all walking with the same slow slump, the same stoop, in the same standard circumstance. But they hold the belief that I should remain an unwelcome blot on their already spoiled landscape.

I have lived here since my parents settled long ago and yet these looks I describe haven't stopped, although it used to be worse than mere looks. In fact, the worst incident I recall was also the first time I had learnt a swear word: cunts. Yes, what a word to discover. Especially when it's smeared blood-red over your front door, the mouth of the letterbox choked. I recall that sore, sharp smack in the face that Mother gave me, for asking what it meant.

I would say, though, that I am almost immune to incidences like these now.

*

I walk into Spar. The cashier acknowledges me with a soft smile, the first I have encountered today. I go towards the magazines. The tabloids scream fear and scandal in bold black. Bodies, either mutilated or airbrushed, sprawl the front pages. I scan the local *Gazette*'s front page.

I notice a chubby-cheeked little girl in a pink duffel coat reaching helplessly for a kids' arts-and-crafts magazine. She outstretches an arm and grabs at it, using another hand to wrench herself up with the aisle's ledge. She tramples on the newspapers. I cannot help but reach out and take one for her.

'Hey,' she then says grumpily, as though I would have stolen it from her.

I hand it to her. I smile but she doesn't see. She snatches it and examines the cover, her eyes bulging and cheeks bunching with her sly smile.

That is until her mother grabs her arm and tries to pull her away: 'Oi, get yer, missus.'

'But I wanna magazine,' pleads the girl, as her mother continues to wrench at her arm. The heavy-handedness is hereditary. 'The lady helped me get it.'

The mother darts her eyes at me. 'Well, you're not having that then,' she says in a low voice. She throws the magazine to the floor towards me and pulls the girl away, shooting her penetrating stare towards me as they go.

I put the magazine back and leave.

*

Only now that I am several yards away from the shop do I realise that I have forgotten to buy anything. I feel shaken and a little sick. Dizzy. For some reason, ashamed. So I keep my eyes to the ground. The grubby floor dappled with dried gum and trampled cigarettes. A pigeon pecks at a discarded sausage roll. Without intention, I startle it from my path. I decide to get the first bus home.

The rusty blue bus shelter is empty, thankfully. I lean on the raised bench and breathe. Suddenly aware that I have no reading material – I was meant to get some in Spar – I begin reading the scrawled, spidery graffiti. POLES GO HOME, BRITAIN FOR BRITS, IAN SUCKS COCK, DIAL FOR SEX, BROWNS GO HOME, HANG THE PEEDOS [sic]. All these voices scream wildly in my head. A Western Wall for sin and prejudice, not to whisper into but to wail.

I see another one towards the bottom. FUCK OFF BANKSY. I laugh.

*

The bus arrives. It is sweltering inside. As the reddening faces of the passengers scan me, I scan for somewhere to sit. There is a window seat at the front next to an innocuous-looking young man who is looking away from me. I perch next to him. I hear a 'tut'. I turn my head and the seat next to me is now empty. I look out the window, into the grey.

We pull up at the next stop and a little old lady gets on, her voice high and loud. Unmistakably Welsh.

'Aw, shit,' she declares, rummaging through her bag. 'Don't tell me I've left that at home now. Oh, *Duw*'.

A tut echoes from the back of the bus.

She addresses the bus: 'Oi, don't you tut at me. We're all in a rush, right?!' I stifle a laugh. 'I am sorry, darlin', how much is it?'

The driver mumbles and she counts out the money in coin. 'There you are, love. Keep the change.'

The doors slip shut.

The only empty seat is next to me. And to my surprise, she takes it, after a slight look at me first. I hear her release a sigh as she sits, as if she were a deflated balloon. I return my gaze to the window, watching the glum houses gawk at whatever's in front of them. I hear the rustle of a magazine and then a cool breeze.

She's fanning herself. 'Christ, ain't you hot in that, love?'

I turn and she's looking at me. Her eyes glimmer, then fade. 'Sorry, I didn't mean anything by that. I just thought… y'know. Must be hot.'

I make a smile that she can't see. I shrug instead. I turn back to the window.

After a moment, she says, 'I've just bought my beach stuff.' I look at her. I wish I could reply. 'Not a bikini, don't worry. I'm going on a cruise round the Caribbean with Roy. I've been on a cruise before, but I spent most of the time over the barriers spewing into the sea.' She lets out a phlegmy cackle, thick as a smoker's.

I want to reply but I don't think I need to.

'I got loads of photos, if you wanna look at em.' She searches through her bag again and snatches out a leopard-print purse that seems to double as a photo album. She flicks through holiday snaps of smiling faces, old and young, her always smiling the same thin-eyed, full-faced grin.

I can't help but grin myself.

'That's my granddaughter, that one. She's about six there; doing her gee-ceeee-sees now or whatever you call 'em. She wants to do nursing, but you know what it's like.' Do I? 'Ah, there's Roy, b'there. Christ, look at that friggin' shirt,' she says, as she lets out another resounding cackle. 'He looks like a right numpty, aye. It'll be forty-two years we been married on Saturday.'

She takes a moment to look at him. I see his similarly full, red cheeks and raised eyebrows. He's eating a kebab but the brown filling has gone all over him. I look back to her and she's still smiling. 'What about your family?' she then asks.

All I can do is shrug. I don't have the words to answer, but I do have a family. I do have origins and memories and all the rest. Not the words, though.

She does not realise the bus has stopped. 'Oh, shit, I'm meant to be off by 'yer. Wait for me, will you!' she shouts to the driver, heaving herself off her seat and rushing to the front. I am somewhat relieved until I see her purse left on the floor, opened to the photo of Roy. I pick it up and run to the doors, but they have closed. I plead to the driver but he doesn't understand and spits, 'Tough.'

I walk back to my seat and nestle the purse into my bag. The woman in the adjacent seat is looking at me, I can feel her, she's looking right at me with this disgusted look on her face because what I'm going to do with the purse is apparently obvious. She's getting her phone out, pointing the camera at me. I have to get off at the next stop.

*

I am home. The silence yawns in my hollow flat. I lay my bags down and get out the purse, flicking through its contents. I am relieved to see her phone number on one of the cards and so I write it on a post-it note. I take off my burqa and dial the number.

Natasha Borton

Cofiwch Dryweryn

Having learnt only to kiss with open lips
and wild tongues
we blew our fingerprints across the dead water.

The arthritics of the lake crack
the memory of youth
home rusts in our hearts.

We clothe the moon with string
spun from the skeleton of lilies
beneath thick cemetery cement.

Will the clouds shed here again?
Will they hear the sigh of the wind over the humming motors?
Fe godwn ni eto.

Natasha Borton

Dadl Dau Mother Story

Wrought iron shadows cut across my cheek as the sun bride peeks from behind blossom net curtains. My mother gave them to me. Along with a thick, moving duvet of goose feathers. They stab each freckle on my shoulder. Tip of the quill poised.

As I write with crimson ink across his pillow. Signatures that carry the dead weight of his name. Eyelashes. For peeking. Singed. Blushing blossom bride comes over the mountain of lace framing her sun beams. She casts watchful eyes as the shadows stretch the backs of tea cups to boulders beneath the bed. Draining leaves of their time and. And the turning of the milk wheels fade away with its

dadl dau, dadl dau dadl dau.

Heels pressed to the boards. The Llygoden scurries in from the shadows. Sips at bitter tea. It's whiskers casting ripples. As the ice melts, dripping. The veins that crack. Shiver and disappear into the. drip. of the. saucer

dadl dau, dadl dau, dadl dau.

Burning fills the house pressing smoking palms against each window. Seeping through the gap in the corner of the room.

Where the Llygoden lives. Seeps and drips, out, into the clean night air. Wrapping around trees and dandelions and

dadl dau, dadl dau, dadl dau.

In dreams he takes me by the wrist. Lifts me from the bed. Duvet melts into glass on the floor. A flock of geese rising to, melting into, the clouds. Her robe curls at the hips and drops from her shoulders. It grows, flows out into the richest river. crimson. Lengths draped from my wrists, as if my arms had been dipped in blood. and I'm dancing, blind, with hands cupped, cups of red before eyes to the shriek of the violins. And I can't stop. Not until I realise that I am the one screaming

dadl dau, dadl dau, dadl dau.

The smoke creeps back, from Llygoden's lungs, as it sips the drops from the robe. It steals, hot like ash, the essence of myself.

Natalie Ann Holborow

Clearing out the single room

I found a thing or ten of yours.
My sister with a stranger's face,
I scrabbled for any piece of you
I could save from the rubble
of your life. Pieced the lost months together
beneath that perilous chandelier
you'd chosen, plastic and shocking pink.
The light shattered into a thousand sequins.

Down on my hands and knees,
I snuffled you out like a pig.
Mascara stained the carpet
as though someone had tripped
in a pair of dirty stilettos,
charring the sticky fibres
of the rug you blazed upon
night after night,
cheap body sprays pressed
to a sickly splutter
to cover your late cigarettes.
Ashes still stuck in a musty fur
at the bottom of every handbag.

It's like one minute you were gone
and then out of nowhere
there you were again,
an oversized child
screaming out of the sock drawer,
the washbasket, howling
at the top of your lungs
from the fug of a dead slipper.
A fake eyelash clings to my finger
and says to me, look, look—
and I see you
clambering out of the boxes,
little girl lost in a dress.

Natalie Ann Holborow

Ed

When my name is called, I sail past them: bunched
like electric wires in their seats, matchstick Lowry girls
pacing green floors, counting calories
on the lengths of their fingers. I feel wide
as an Atlas among them. I have learned the latitudes
of my thighs, the altitude of each breast.
Ed comes with me, screaming.

Ed doesn't have a body.
Most mornings, over black coffee
and Marlboro, slim ribbons of chemical blues,
he had me naked and shivering,
inspecting every mirror. We frowned then,
lengthened the rope of my spine
to a chain of pearls. It wouldn't do.
I ran for miles in the snow.

Sometimes now I talk, crawl out of this odd shape
like some half-born animal, talk about Ed
until he fades to a medical term –
the therapied grey-matter headache.
They pin him to a clipboard,
handwrite his Latin name.
Ed dies weighing less than a skeleton.

Natalie Ann Holborow

Smokers' Lane

Smokers' Lane goes back and down
like a throat about to spit.
Branches, slick-black, prod my shadow;
lead them to me like jackals.
In corridors, they press me
but still, they do not know me,
even after four slow years
where my silence and my clever pen
have rocked them senseless with laughter.
They see me, glittering with sovereigns
tight around nicotined fingers.

Skirt-tugging, creamy thighs
spread on cracking walls—
Look at us! A-D-U-L-T-S,
collars skewed like dead birds, cigarettes jutting,
pissed at ten in the morning. Uniformed,
hair tucked back, I pass their rasping laughter,
blush at the fall of my name. Wet stones.
Gold studs rattle bad teeth.

The three o'clock crawl to the gate.
I am wading knee-deep through dogshit now,
through smoked-out names—*fucking swot*—

stinking my clothes out for days.
Quietly, I carry my words out like secret friends
they would trample and burn in the lane.

Miriam Elin Jones

Winged Creatures

Fucking seagulls. Literally, fucking seagulls. Fucking all the bloody time. This time of year, they didn't stop. I couldn't do anything but lie there and listen to them, having been unlucky enough to end up in the attic room.

They squawked and screeched, louder and louder and louder as they did it. Do birds thrust like humans do? I wasn't sure. I'd never actually seen them at it. Watching them would be rude, after all. That morning, I listened to them reach their ultimate crescendo, every piercing cry pinching my sore head, until they flew away.

The sex bit was easy. It was working out what it meant and what came next that complicated things. Did they make love or just make babies? Were they flying off in different directions or heading off together, sweeping over the sea to greet the horizon?

It was no wonder I'd slept with someone else. The seagulls had driven me to it. Watching my boyfriend, who was over a hundred miles away, wanking on Skype had long lost its novelty.

And now That Someone Else – whom I'd only met in Pier Pressure the night before – was trying to sneak out. He was the multi-coloured man, glowing under the strobe lighting. His edges were blurred, as if he was an apparition rather than human. Who knows how it started – I was drunk – but all I remember is slow dancing to a fast song, because that made sense at the time.

Had I told him about Matt?

He got up that morning and hadn't prepared himself for the sloping ceiling. How was he to know? He couldn't remember how he'd gotten there, let alone the dimensions of the room. He banged his head and cursed. Of course he'd tried to make a run for it. I couldn't keep pretending he wasn't there. Because he was, even though he definitely shouldn't be. I knew I had to face him – he'd already stumbled over my easel and was swearing loudly. I didn't want the others to know anyone was here.

I opened my eyes.

He was suddenly solid in the morning light. A human being rather than a ghost, despite being as pale as a blank piece of paper. He was tall and lanky and every jutting bone of his skinny frame was in perfect focus. He was real. A fact. There. I couldn't deny or pretend it wasn't happening. I watched him rifle through my dirty laundry pile with one hand, nursing the bump on his head with the other.

I uttered the first thing that came to mind: 'Do you want a cup of tea?'

He stopped in his tracks and turned to stare at me, horrified. 'I can't find my fucking pants.'

'It doesn't matter.'

'It does if I want to get out that door.'

'Where did you take them off?'

'I can't even remember your name, luv, as if I can fucking remember that.'

I'm sure he was courteous last night.

Hadn't we sat on one of those benches along the prom and talked? I'd probably told him everything. About me. About my work. My life. My boyfriend. Someone Else (I never learnt his name, despite letting him fuck me senseless) had tried to tell me about himself too, but I didn't want to know.

That morning, he left, forgetting his pants but taking my secrets with him.

*

I loved watching the starlings. Forming new, dark clouds and enticing people to watch them dance. What would happen if a lone seagull was caught amongst them? The poor thing having been swept along in the tide of birds, a clumsy, white blob, like a shit stain splattered on a freshly cemented pavement.

I'd heard someone say that it was the starlings that made Aberystwyth special, as if it was the only thing the place had going for it. Of course, that someone had pair of binoculars around his neck and a neatly trimmed moustache. No one was going to take him, of all people, seriously. There were many things that made Aber special. It takes all sorts of things – and people – to make a place special.

I concentrated harder than usual on the starlings and thought about the imaginary seagull stuck amongst them. Struggling to keep afloat, pushing against them all and trying to be free.

'You're not mad, are you?' Matt. Interrupting my thoughts, forcing me to face him.

Of course I was. But I couldn't say anything. Even I knew I was being unreasonable.

'You are?'

'No,' I replied unconvincingly.

'You understand though, right?'

I did. I couldn't blame him for moving away. Didn't blame him at all. There were opportunities in Cardiff. Jobs. More than just salt water, students and an unhealthy amount of pubs. The chorus of chirping starlings above my head couldn't distract me for long. I'd seen them a million times before, and my mind wandered. Matt wouldn't see these in the capital. Just plenty of dirty pigeons.

Would he miss the birds? Would he miss me?

'I know you won't go...'

'Can't go,' I corrected.

'Won't...'

We both knew how stubborn I could be.

'But we'll be okay. You can come for holidays. Date nights in Cardiff Bay. It'll be nice.'

Because our life here wasn't. I thought he'd be around to see my first exhibition appear at the Gas Gallery. At least. If not stick with his supermarket job and get by, as I was doing. Instead, he was disappearing to a better paid 'professional' job at the Welsh Assembly.

'Maybe you'll be ready to come too sometime...?'

He knew I wasn't going anywhere. I didn't want to disappear amidst a maze of terraced streets in Cardiff and be forced to paint dull houses and big shopping centres. I couldn't bear the thought of spending a fortune going from club to club every night to drown my sorrows.

That was just too easy.

I wasn't going.

'There are more...'

Breaks? Yes. Possibly. But twice as many wannabes too, all fighting for gallery space and dressing in ridiculously garish jumpers in order to create a personality to get noticed. It wasn't like that here. There weren't enough people to hide amidst and I could be me. Just me.

The starlings nestled on their winter home, under the pier, as Matt and I sat there in silence. Could the seagull go with them? You know, that seagull in my mind that had mistakenly joined them. Was it time for the seagulls to migrate too? Leave Aber, and let the tourists eat their chips in peace. But I had that sinking feeling that the seagull knew he didn't belong. He wasn't one of them.

*

I didn't tell Matt about the man from Pier Pressure. Not that he was a real man. He was at that awkward age where he was too old to be a boy, but too young to be a man. Mid-twenties. I just hoped he wasn't local – I never asked – and that I wouldn't bump into him again. Anyway, Matt didn't need to know.

It was almost time for my monthly visit to Cardiff and I was dreading the four hour train journey more than ever. I'd seen the rolling Welsh countryside plenty of times before and I always ended up sitting by someone with bad body odour (well, not always, but more often than not). Matt had begun to complain I was always miserable. Complaining about everything. I was too tired and too skint to do anything 'fun'. I'd be worse this time. I was an awful liar.

Having stripped the bedsheets and done my laundry, I wandered out, through the castle and towards the Old College, drawn towards the sea. Somehow, watching the waves stroke the pebbled beach calmed me. It was starling time again and they flew above my head. Funny, how time flew. Not quite as gracefully, but just as fast. They were back again – not that many people noticed they weren't there. No one made a fuss. They just weren't there and that was that. Less of a risk of being shat on, and the cameras stopped clicking. Nobody takes pictures of the lonely seagulls begging tourists for crumbs, even though they're just as much a part of this town too. In fact, they should be more a part of the town than the starlings. They never leave.

I'd treated myself to fish and chips for supper, but I didn't really fancy them in the end. I'd lost my appetite, along with my dignity. I left them resting on the overflowing litter bin… and I'd barely walked away when a seagull plunged from the sky, and began feasting on the chips I couldn't stomach. I felt sick, knowing that very seagull had probably been perched on the roof of my house, probably listening to me having sex with someone else, just as I'd been listening to them.

I hated them. Fucking seagulls. The chalk to the starlings' cheese. It was never going to work, was it? Yet, I couldn't stay angry. Someone - whether it was God, Allah or a crazy scientist in a laboratory - had created the seagulls for a reason. Somebody had to stay behind, after all.

Mari Ellis Dunning

Shedding

We can't jar mismatched pieces, make them fit;
too many days, months, years, already wasted.
You may have given me your face, peeled it
like pastry from your smoking skull, and pasted
it to my small ivory head instead; but you
never drew ink along the dotted line.
Years handpicking fathers like flowers – true,
you were no daffodil, certainly not mine.
They're calling us to boarding finally,
I leave my suitcase standing on the platform –
a twenty-one year wait or so it seems.
Like you, I won't be back. Excuses worn.
I've shed that second skin; the coat I'd sewn
and stapled to my back, too small, outgrown.

Mari Ellis Dunning

The Red Balloon

lifts
        slowly
                        carried on a breeze
gentle as a child's morning breath.
It sways mid-air, a ballet dancer
breathing in, gathering a lungfull
then gathering its guts. It topples,
takes off in a gust, unconfined,
and shares its secrets with the wind.

ii.

The red balloon sails away
until it becomes a speck, no more
than colourless dust. I can't see
my note anymore, but I know
that it trails unwillingly on string,
It may end the day in a tangle of branches -
for cheap thrills, I'll take my chances.

iii.

The red balloon is just out
of grasp, it taunts me, gliding

like a cartoon ghost and skirting
my eager fingers. Weighted,
it ducks and dodges, disappears
over the tracks with one final dive
out of reach, gone, it could be alive.

iv.

The red balloon was lodged in the gorse
depleted, sad, wrinkled like elephant skin.
I thought of a crying child, a clown,
and reached for its umbilical string,
dragged it free, pulled it screaming, found
a golden band, a note neatly folded in four –
'I can't be this person anymore.'

Erin Mathias

Joy

Driving is easy for Jacob because he grew up on a farm, and every farmer's son will learn to drive a tractor as early the law allows to take the strain away from a father's aching day. Freshly teenaged he was. His father, leather limbs, hands like tools, joints bulging, with the arcs of his nails a bed full of oil, toil and turf, moved his own milky, freckle-speckled hands to all the right places.

At seventeen, he had no trouble passing his driving test: two lessons, he had, and no minors, something that impressed the girls in his *dosbarth cofrestru*. No way, they gasped, controlling the bubble gum in their mouths, doodling in sickly bubble writing on each other's arms. It impressed his parents less. At home, his father didn't even look up and his mother's eyes were quartered lemons facing down towards her thick knitting needles. To this day, he does not own a car.

But now, as sun glitters the C road ahead, he feels lucky that his job allows him to drive a van. It swells as he lifts it over the lump and slows and rolls it around the slate workshop, into third, and into the sparse village of Llangatwyn.

She is waiting for him in her deckchair, as she did on Saturday, Friday, Thursday, every day but the holy day. She hasn't taken the curlers out of the frizzy white yet and is reading a copy of *Chat*. Jacob remembers sitting in the room *ffrynt*, and how his mother always read the stories about the men who hurt their wives or killed their children or stole the children but when his father came in to the room she would flick quick to the crossword, furrow her brow and chew on her prop. She was sharper back then.

Jacob carries the bag of post up the path. He smiles at Joy and Joy smiles back. He removes her envelopes and as their hands meet, he notices how neat she looks, pastel jumper clashing with the tired lines in her arms and through her hands. Painted are her nails, today a bluey-green.

'Thank you, Jacob. A fine day to be sat outside, is it not?'

Although the sun is warm, the wind beats at his trousers, and he looks at her bare legs, the varicose veins shimmering bulges. He wishes she'd cover them up. It's cold. Poor Joy. 'Beautiful, Joy.'

'*Odi glei*, Jacob. How is your father in the Big House? Please send him my regards.'

'He is well.'

'That's good to hear.'

*

He goes to visit his old dad. As he passes the window he gives it the soft, familiar knock.

His father gives back that soft, familiar cry: 'Jacob?' He is in his chair and his shirt, some type of check, hangs loosely forward with the bend of his back. He looks old, like a hawk, everything but the chair he sits in a callous, cold surrounding, the smell of medicine and potatoes boiling on the stove.

Without a word, Jacob moves to the kettle to make tea – one teabag between two, because weak is what we like here.

His dad's hands rattling makes Jacob's smile wince and

force a face into his cup. He scrapes his chair back with the back of his legs and gets up from the table without looking up and he walks upstairs.

His mother's old room is empty like a shell; just one chest of drawers, its contents left for the moths, to avoid the misery of moving them. Jacob reaches down to the top drawer and, in there, he sees what he came for: a pair of thick woollen tights. They'll be good for Joy, he thinks. She will like these, just as his mother did.

'I'll be going soon now,' he says.

'OK, Jacob. Jacob, it was nice to see you. Tell me now, how are you?'

'I'm OK, Dad. *Iawn. Dwi'n iawn.*'

'Have you any luck with the women?' And at the clunkiness of the question he opens his mouth to smile and the white sticky spit reveals itself fast like plague because Jacob's father smiles little these days. 'I know I am not the most fun person to ask but I do think of you sometimes, a lot of times in a day, you see.' He coughs and bile runs up his throat and he grimaces and swallows it down.

Jacob does not take his eyes off his father. His father sips the cooling tea.

'I'm well Dad,' and he reaches into his pocket bulging with tights and repeats: 'I'm okay.'

'Okay, it was nice for you to come.'

The father is glad when Jacob is gone; he has something he's been planning do.

*

The journey to Carmarthen is long, and it is one he hasn't taken in years. He is going to buy a laptop for Jacob. He doesn't really know what a laptop means but Janet Down Shop told him her son has one and spends all his time speaking with friends on it, even on the weekend. Be nice for you to spend some money on the boy, she said. It's what she'd have wanted, she said.

The muggy greyness of outside spills into the insides of the shop, but for the gaudy, slippery screens.

'You all right there?' says a boy with more gum than tooth.

'Thank you, yes. I am looking for a laptop.'

'What kind of features are you looking for? Windows? We don't sell Macs here.'

'I am looking for a laptop for my son so that he can speak with his friends on it.'

The boy smiles then, pants higher than trousers, turns and walks towards another member of staff.

The other employee is older and wears a tie and his hair looks wet. He comes over. 'Hello, Sir. I hear you are looking for a laptop for your son. This is our most popular one. This is our biggest seller. It's got everything your son would need.'

'Can he speak with friends through it?'

'Yes, he can do that on this laptop, sure.' The man smiled with his fat lips.

'Okay.'

'Great! I'll take it over to the checkout for you.'

As they pass the young colleague the important man winks and put his thumbs up.

'That'll be £699 please.'

Jacob's father looks up from his wallet. He moves his hand to his bank card and it shakes. He puts his four numbers in, clutches the bag to his chest, and begins the long walk back to the bus stop.

The employees watch him leave, and the eldest grins: 'Here comes this month's bonus!'

*

February's sky is awake as she hands out the day's gift: crisp, cloudless sky and dew ready to be rid. The landscape – *cwm, twmpath, nant* – all skip past Jacob and the mountains, arching away from him, roll and roll like a turn of phrase.

She isn't waiting for him. She isn't in her deck chair. He knocks. She doesn't answer. He knows. He drops the tights, turns around, gets back in the van, drives over the river, stops the van, takes his heavy bag of post, dumps its contents in the river, screams up into the sky, gets back in the van, drops off the van and walks to his dad's, still in uniform.

'Joy, Jacob...' Jacob's father's words dissolve and he watches his son sitting cross-legged in the wooden ladder-back chair, thumb at his mouth, sucking lightly like a lamb. He will wait till another day to give him his present.

*

As the seasons fall through the hourglass Jacob still comes each day with the dawn to his duty. He still visits his joy, treading the path to her door, miming handing her post. One Saturday, the children across road see him on his knees, face-first in the turf, battering down, each sob catching up with the next, and there he stays for eight whole minutes.

That day, when Jacob returns, a box is on his doorstep:

Here for you is a laptop, all set up,
so all you must do is turn it on.
They set up email so you can speak
with your friends.
Dad.

Jacob makes room on the table and opens his new laptop, moving it delicate, scared his big soft hands will damage its smooth black back. Outside, night falls asleep and Jacob is alone, lit by the screen. Outside, birds speak to each other, wind whips the air and maybe a fox screeches. He clicks: New Message. Where it says To he types: JOY EVANS, 4 BONT FACH, LLANGATWYN, DYFED, SA33 0LW. He then clicks in the big empty space below and lets it all out.

Kitty May Howell Jones

The Eldest Alone

Oh little one,
little madam,
little bitch.
You know your crime and
you will hang by the neck.
For a shining ten penny, you'll swing.

I will dance around you like a maypole,
flicking at your small Oxford soles.
Myself remaining unflicked,
unpoked, unprodded, untattle-taled.
Naught short of a mouse, in its small,
mouse house.

You loved the velvet heads…

Should I wish you back?
Undance the dance I skipped around your heart?
I'll knock,
try again,
rap once more?

I'll see you in another place, little me.

Emily Green

It's not AnghaRUD, it's AnghaRAD

'She looks like the love child of Katherine Jenkins and that pretty boy off *This Morning,* what's he called? Matt something. He came to our school in some Welsh boyband a few years ago, terrible they were! Gave you a cheeky snog though didn't he 'Chelle!'

'Fuck off did he, gave me more than that he did!'

All the girls were pissing themselves laughing. It was funny, they were funny, and everything on Nitrous Oxide was fucking hysterical. That summer went on forever, its sticky trail oozing its way through the valley and on to next door's disposable barbecue. It stank the village out, congealed steaks peppered with blood for the men, and plastic sausages off the back of Gaz's van for their women.

'Bet you like that love, all in one!'

'Shut your trap Benji, she'd eat you alive, good boy!'

Jenna Johnson took her hotdog to those perfect parted lips she had, and ate it in one go. She was amazing. We'd watch her through the hole in 'Chelle's fence, as she gorged on pork covered in cheap starch, silver painted eyelids reflecting the throbbing sun right back into our perving eyes. She was always smiling, even if the pricks with tribal bands around their biceps and vests with yellow patches under their curly armpits were bothering her. Angharad's mam babysat Jenna when she was just an agglomeration of chubby fists and bleeding gums. She told us to stay away from her because she paints her fingernails red and files them to a stiletto point, and we all know what that means. She's religious though, so we don't bother listening half the time.

Angharad always knew she was going to be a hairdresser. Her mam went nuts on her when she found out on results day that she hadn't bothered to turn up for half of her GCSEs, doodling on the rest of them. Big, fat hearts with Kieran in the middle. He had a car that he'd take her round the Mc Donald's drive-thru in on a Friday night. She never bothered with a condom, but said she wouldn't catch anything, 'cause only slags get chlamydia when they don't wash.

'No daughter of mine is living on minimum wage for the rest of her life!'

'Chill Mam, I'm going to have my own business one day, I'll pay myself a wage.'

She was proper triumphant after her delivery, but not so much when she was met with a handprint tattooed on her sunburnt face for being a cheeky cow. We went in Kieran's car down the cast because she needed to give some of the girls a trim. She gave him a slow, wet kiss when she got out of his modified Corsa. I kept my eye on his plump cold sore that her bottom lip kept catching, fluid wriggling around under the skin.

Angharad didn't bother charging me anymore. She was going to do it full time in September, taking BTEC hair and beauty in our local college, even though she'd been doing her Barbies since she was six. 'Chelle didn't do well in her exams either, too busy poking boys on Facebook and watching make-up tutorials on YouTube to care about *Of Mice and Men*.

'Why don't she just leave him, Sir? Curly sounds like a right twat!'

'You're going to look like a right twat if you don't buck your ideas up, Michelle Williams!'

She was okay though, her dad was loaded, made plastic cups for a living or something, spending the week living up in Cardiff. When we turned eighteen, she promised us we'd go there and have a proper night out, where we could get food afterwards, and places stayed open until at least 3am.

I was going to college too, one of the only ones to do my A levels. 'Chelle told me it was because I was brainy, but Angharad said it was because I was English like my mam, where they teach you proper things, not just Welsh and how to rear sheep.

'Good job you don't sound like that anymore mind, all posh! They'd piss themselves in Bridgend Col if they'd heard you a few years back!'

'Shut your mouth or I won't bother writing any more of your shit haircuts down! Now hurry up or I'll dob you into the tax office, you bloody moonlighter!'

When we weren't supervising Angharad's amateur cuts down the cast, we'd be on our backs, our heads below blackberries that hung and clotted in the bushes, blistering pockets of blood staining our fingers when we pulled our leggings back up. Nobody went to college a virgin. Tom was my first of many that summer, the only one that didn't announce that I wasn't frigid down the rugby club. Stunning he was, with a gap between his teeth and a job up in Swansea. He was older, see.

They usually were.

'Chelle lost her v-plates when she was thirteen, and was a pro in getting what she wanted, her laugh tinkling in the boys' ears like some magical voodoo. She'd always end up with the fittest one, dropping her home afterwards. I'd have to walk back, sticky thighs rubbing together with the beginnings of a Strongbow hangover. Dad never suspected anything from his little *pili-pala*, but mam wouldn't look me in the eye after she'd done the washing, blood-stained pants mixed with snail trails from Tom or Ollie or Dan.

'There's nothing beautiful about being the village butterfly, though.' She'd say bike when Dad wasn't around, but he ignored her anyway, turning the page of his tabloid over; another defeat for City.

It happened on the night of Llanfawr's fair; historically, an occasion for us to celebrate not getting knocked up before our sixteenth birthdays, but traditionally, another opportunity to get bollocksed and throw up on your mate's knock-off handbag from Turkey. That illuminated phallic machine would tower over us as we exchanged pocket money for polystyrene cups of White Lightning, and a quick hand-job for rollies. I still can't stand the smell of burning sugar, its fluffy pink exterior stuffed into vacuum bags, trapped until some mug takes it home in exchange for half hour's wage. Angharad had already been on half the rides, teeth marks punched into the side of her cup from where she'd been juggling her fags with a cone of oily chips.

'Where've you been? We've already gone on half the rides, and 'Chelle's gone with some div that works on the Teacups.'

'Give me a chance woman, I've had enough earache off mam for not taking the rubbish out last night, I don't need you yapping in my ear too. We gonna get 'Chelle, or is she a lost cause?'

'Lost cause, probably gone back to his caravan. Hold this will you, I need to sort my shoe out, it's been giving me jip all night!'

I held onto her stupid plastic bag for hours, the half-drunk bottles inside knocking my ankles whilst she had her mouth inside Kieran's smug face. Kelly Cuckoo kept trying to talk to me, offering me a lick of her ice-cream that she whipped up to a perfect point with her pink tongue. She didn't drink, see. It messed her tablets up or something, and she seemed happy enough nodding her head to the music blasting from the plastic machines, spilling their neon hues over the usually desolate wasteland.

I left her to find Angharad, who wasn't difficult to locate, her left thigh draped over Kieran, blowing grey smoke into some idiot's face. He put his hands on her arse and slapped it. She didn't mind, but I decided I finally did. They were crawling all over her, muddy prints rubbing on creased denim; fat, pink flesh in her symmetrical pockets. I tried taking her away but she wasn't having any of it, because I was just a jealous cow that couldn't even get a boyfriend.

'Have it your way then, Ang, but I'll fucking remember this.'

I cut through the trees down by where the old Kwik-Save used to be, swinging the contents of the bag I'd been holding all night until the handles snapped. The final vein of plastic gave way as a muffled yell thread its way through the shrubbery. I knew it was her, the flash of black hair whipping the car window as he pulled back on her arm. I'd heard stories, but everybody knows that you can't trust Fat Brenda from the chippy. Everyone does it down there, you get used to it after a while, and it's no longer funny to hide behind the car and smack on the window when the bobbing heads get louder, but she didn't look bored, or happy, or on the brink of a massive orgasm. Jenna Johnson looked over at me with a soggy face and red arm, mouthing at me with those perfect lips to come over.

But I didn't bother, I just kept walking.

Sara Robles

To Frida

You in a cast
in a blue house,

your mother brings an easel,
your father brings a brush.

You paint
what you see,
what is real

to you.

Then
a bed of pain
and a monkey

wraps you in his tail,
as he has before,
and you climb
the branches and the cords;
you find your babies.

Meanwhile, we hear someone's wife died –
a painter's. Years later, we remember

your eyes and your pictures.
I think yours were better.

Would there be paint
on the canvas or the wood,
the metal or the copper plates,

would I know your strong face

had you not been raped
by the iron rail of that bus?

Chelsea Gilmore

You & I

I thought my hands were small until I watched yours drum the sticky table, bar smoke hanging low around your head.

You could barely keep eye contact in the beginning and when you did I could see them working, wondering which mutual friend had guilted me into sitting here with you.

In truth, I'd always admired you so it came as no surprise when our group of friends suggested that we go out somewhere on our own. They said you could use a girl like me and made it sound like I'd be doing you some colossal favour, but I knew I'd need you just as much as you'd need me.

You'll hate that admission. You'll hate the word 'admire' because it comes with the word 'despite' each time it's used around you. 'Despite' your illness, 'despite' the wheelchair, 'despite' the whole damn lot of it. I know and I'm sorry.

The pub was your choice. You said that The Arms made you feel too old and joked that your bones did that well enough on their own. You said that the outdated furniture and faded patterned carpets could make even your wheelchair look youthful. We laughed but I caught the sting in your eye all the same.

You settled on the Fourtrees even though their disabled access wasn't up to scratch. I found it too dark but the furniture was up-to-date as was the music and I could tell that it satisfied you through your unease. We took a table in a corner and I read over the names scratched into the dark table as you shifted your chair into place and kept your back to the rest of the room.

Twenty minutes in, I saw your wrist poking out from under your bulked-up biker jacket and asked if you weren't too warm. You shifted uncomfortably before letting it fall from your shoulders and watched me notice the awkward way your button-up shirt clung around your body. You shrugged then, cocked your head and smirked to see how I'd deal with it.

Okay. I can't say I wasn't conscious of the way your shoulders jutted from their sockets and I'd always been aware of the way your shirt stumbled over ridge after ridge of your curling spine. But I didn't flinch and held your dark stare, nodding as your straining neck forced your eyes from mine. 'I'll fetch the drinks' I said, standing abruptly.

Looking back to our table, I noticed a faint tremor in your right arm and wondered if scotch could really be considered a mixer for muscle relaxants. I still wonder that now when I see you, necking it back easily, shot for shot, pill for pill.

'So a Politics degree, huh?' I said, sitting back down. You nodded. 'And Criminal Justice as a minor?'

'How's it going?' I asked.

'You mean considering I've been at it four years already? Super.' You rolled your eyes back, choking the scotch down dramatically.

'Yes,' I surprised you, 'yes, considering you've been at it four years, on and off.' I'd grown impatient with your sarcasm. 'Something must be keeping you there. So tell me for God's sake, why the fuck you love politics.'

You looked me in the eye then, startled from your depressed haze and laughed. It was a loud, barking laugh that was half cynical, half release and I laughed too.

Thirty-six hospital appointments, 156 bottles of scotch and a year later, I sat at the foot of your bed.

'What time is your flight?' you asked, softened to me now. I broke eye contact to look out of your window and sighed. I didn't want to say goodbye.

'9am,' I finally choked, my throat tight. 'I better…'

'Go home and pack Fresher,' you stated simply. 'I'll see you to the door.'

I winced then and reached for your wheelchair. It was sterile, sad and looked like the hospital and I knew my final image of you couldn't include it. I looked back at you as you lay in your pillow cocoon. The various flumps of feathery white fleshed you out and for a moment you looked healthy.

'Stay there' I urged quietly. 'I can see myself out. Only—'

'—Just go. I mean, hey, I'm self-absorbed but I'm no idiot. I said I'd never jump into someone's life and here I am. Don't look offended, love, but you didn't break my rules. You were just an exception to them and it's time you got your distance. Do what I can't and remember, I couldn't go anywhere if I tried.'

There was nothing more to say. I stood and took your hand, squeezed it softly and turned. I clicked your bedroom door shut behind me and made my way home knowing that the first and most complicated of my goodbyes had been completed.

The muscular atrophy settled in soon after I left.

Your arms rippled, vascular red into your hands and raised your pale fingers against your white cell minority.

You laughed bitterly in those days as you watched your sinew cut clean. 'Let's face it,' you'd say, 'there was no muscle to begin with.'

Your dark humour had taken you over but when you appeared each night on my computer screen, head awkwardly bobbing, you'd pulled your sleeves down from the elbows and added layer to layer of clothing.

You kept our conversations polite and work-focused so much so that I couldn't ask what had been done to you. Being so far away, I couldn't see. I got a sense of it in bits and pieces that filtered through your jokes.

'You could mistake me for robot below the waist.' You were fond of that one.

You kept contact, though some days were harder than others and you soon learned to cover your silence with sporadic links to Youtube videos.

I started to read too much into them. I substituted the words of singers like Sam Cooke, Talking Heads, Black Box Recorder for yours when I knew realistically that you just kind of liked Duran Duran.

As the bad days piled up around us, our playlist grew and every now and then I'd slip a song in for myself.

Yeah. You'll find it uncomfortable that I remember. You'll find it more uncomfortable still when I say that I know what you're like. I do.

You've got me thinking about all that. Did I ever really get that distance?

I'm a third year student now but when I'm sitting in class, how much of my head is with you? How much of me is hovering around the hospital bed, scared to lean over and see how much thinner your skin can spread?

I'm unsure of what has brought me here to watch the broken pixels that make up your face stutter through a bad Skype connection. However thin our connection wears it has been the only constant in my life this last four years.

I don't know how to answer your words that I've left to die with the static on my speakers.

'You must love me.' I think you surprised us both.

I could laugh it off or change the subject.

No. The pause has been too long for that.

You could be right, I suppose. Three years of sympathy would be too much for anyone and that isn't what this is. I'm finding it hard to give a name to the situation that I've found myself in. I can carry you up the stairs and I can wheel you into surgeries and white knuckle it until they're over. Hell, I've done it enough times over the last few years.

But can I acknowledge that as my life?

I've never been great with 'boy trouble' or 'relationship drama' and I'm not even sure that's what we're facing. Do all relationships struggle with physicality? Is a relationship defined by physical closeness? Looking back on our time together, I'm not sure that it is.

I think you said it best a few years ago when you said, 'You're it. The *only* it. I don't know what 'it' is. But you're it.'

I'm following from the worried lines around your eyes to your pointed cheek bones that seem to hold your whole face upright and I've reached the cusp.

'You're right, you know. I *must* love you.'

Sam Graydon

On 'Abroath Abbey', by John Piper

Senses of guilt that well up
From the fenland of the heart
Spread out, wandering outward,
Flatly, drowning the debris of
   Their beginning -

Of having never achieved
Feeling more profound than, vague
Inadequacy, fatal myopia,
The old bones of the Abbey -
And I brook my disappointment -
Say Nothing which they said to
   Him - the artist -

I am become a second
And not a little prolix in this passage,
So thought is as the inked night,
A sense of imposed feeling -
Vast and infinite, my own
Overtaken white ruin
Stands alone met by the moonlight
   A sense sublime -

Expelled lightning cracks within
The mind's gospel of wild clouds,
I cannot shorten my response
I cannot hold on the sluice -
The mire will come, all-fearing
The future, Posterity -
Should it ever come - is not mine
   But a spirit

Who will sell you to the ink -
Black night, the remaining bones
Of History, the stones, stood
Out amongst the artist's strokes.
History is a marshland, floating
   Periphrasis,

Verbose exchange of thought,
So, mixing clouds with Abbey
Until God is no longer
A match for his own Terror
And I have no more words.

Ianto Jones

I'm Sure I'm Dying

Outside,
    they puff
    plumes
        of cloud-smoke

inside,
    I feel
    the greenhouse
heat

of the windows;
    sure that I'm
dying.
    Or, at least,

at the end
    of a slow,
slow
    demise.

The pain
    in my side
kept me up
    again
    last night;

a swollen
storm
that raged
and made
me
as lethargic
and pathetic
as the breeze.

But
the ethanol
goes down
easy as air.

Ianto Jones

Debris after Death

He turned as they burned the body
and cried in private, under late, unbridled
sunlight. Then night turned nausea to numb,
drunk-memories and debris after death.
They moved between the green terrace garden,
the kitchen and oblivion and over-told
a life; whose years, through tears, tentatively,
were relived. They returned; I learned, in the last
of evening, sunlight growing, something of grief.

Durre S. Mughal

Here's how it Happens

My hand suspends above the door handle. I check the time, check the date, check for keys, money, shoes. Check I haven't got my shirt on wrong or half tucked in my pants. Check my laces are tied and my feet aren't dragging discarded tissue paper. Check my reflection.

Check my reflection.

The old clock ticks audibly in the hallway. I continue to stare, ready to go, to step out of the door but there is tomorrow, or the next day. I don't need to go out today. Maybe it is too late now anyway. I imagine the bus passing my stop as I get to it. Alone in the hallway, the eyes that I have no control over, that will meet mine as soon as I step out, bore through me. The sound of car horns, traffic fumes, and angry mothers shielded behind prams come to me as I stand with my hand above the latch. I decide not to go.

In the night I rub my cold feet between the covers and the mattress as if to light a spark, a fire to burn down the numbness that has crept into my body. My eyes dampen and I'm shouting FUCK FUCK FUCK FUCK but the sound doesn't get past my temples to my mouth. Instead it builds up like waves slamming repeatedly against the concrete walls of a hollow room. I draw my legs up to my chest, cross my arms and rock my head to even out the pressure in my temples.

That's how it happened the first time. Ten days of doing just that. It used to be easy, this stepping out of the door. It wasn't something I had to think about. It didn't linger around, need planning around to be done. Yet when it happened I couldn't really say much. It came subtly, slowly, like the change that comes at a certain point in the night. It is not the sky changing colours or people going to sleep. It comes way after that. Way after the silence, and before the break of dawn. It is like the silence deepens, and as you focus on it, it grows quieter still. The night is at its thickest then. As though it passes through another realm, and in that short time we pass through a tunnel, a black hole that stills and silences everything like a vacuum. Then at 5.30am you hear the dawn. There is a noise as the world turns over. The sun pulls back the black across the sky and you can hear that too. It is a low, subdued note. You have to hear it to know it.

But that was how it came. Like the subtle vacuum of the night and I couldn't say much because it wouldn't have made sense. But I felt it. I wasn't tired but I felt tired. I was hungry but midway through my plate I felt full. My sister and I were having lunch. I remember looking up at her and seeing a distance in her eyes. She had been distracted too. Inverted. A strip of inner monologue was running across her forehead. I wanted to talk to someone. I wanted to scream and beg for some understanding, for some recognition of what was happening— what was happening to me? But at the time I bent my head over the plate and ate in silence. It was easy. You scrape the bits of rice onto your spoon. Put the spoon in your mouth. You chew and mix the rice with your spit until you're ready to swallow. The chewing prepares your throat for it, so it is easier. And then you swallow. And then repeat.

I couldn't bring myself to go to the doctor's at first and tell them how I was feeling. Or be put on pills that would mess with you, or be on long waiting lists for something that could just be a phase. It was lazy, dramatic. I just had to chin up a bit. My mother also thought that there was nothing drastically wrong with me. She was suspicious of doctors and the 'dog' that she said was chasing after me whenever I got panic attacks. She herself had missed many therapy sessions and look at her, she was fine right? In our house, the odd ghostly voice in the room didn't mean you were insane and had to admit yourself like a psycho. It meant there really could be an intruder, giving you that cold, breaking that dish, giving you bad luck. No, the psychos were the ones who went to the doctor's and ignored the ghostly signs. She would say, it's too late for me now but I'm not having my daughters like this. No, you gotta chin up. You gotta get yourself out of it. And so I never went because it would mean that the 'dog' had gotten me too.

But then you start slipping up. Sleeping in later, staying up later. Getting ill for the first time in years. Your own body betrays you. Your mouth, stunned in the day yet loud as a cat in heat at night, blurts out the nightmares you don't want others to see. You start to set yourself reminders to shower and the part time job you bear becomes unbearable.

*

Monday. Driving on Penylan Hill. The road is empty but for the sedentary cars parked on the sides. The light from the sun filters through the trees. We are at the top, rolling down, but when we reach the bottom the peace turns into a sharp silence and I think, where has this come from? Where has all the air gone? In that moment, the silence turns into a menace that comes down on me. I feel its presence even though I know the menace is all inside me. And me inside the car with its windows rolled up tight, air tight, with us shut in and I can't breathe. I won't be able to breathe even if they are rolled down. I want out. Out of the line, out of the belt strapped tight against my stomach. The glass shows the outside from the inside of the car like a false promise. It doesn't feel real; a poster someone will take down any moment. I had better keep this to myself. I had better not say anything, do anything. This journey will soon be over. If I bolt she will know, she will tell, and they will know. And definitely no air for me then.

At night I lie with my head pushed down hard into the foam, with just the sound of the silence. Unknown names run across my eyes, jumping like baboons in a cage, this one, that one, staring with their eyes, making that racket. Stop that racket. Stop that racket you. I let them play, let them jump around, hoping that this will make them happy. Silently I am trying to reach God. I say, God God God God God. But God is too far away from me and I am left with the baboons in my head.

*

I start writing it down. Vow to do it in a notebook not to be taken seriously. It will not mean anything; no one will see it, and no one will read it. It will be separate from the 'real' writing. I also vow to never read back through it in case I rip any of the pages out.

A few weeks later I leave work, guiltily, necessarily, reminding myself of what is important, what I had lost sight of. I set myself writing goals and go to more meetings to make sure I don't forget it this time.

I keep a pen specifically for that other notebook, and after I'm done, I hook it into its binders before putting the notebook at the back of my shelf.

Kevin Hudson

Fingerless

A cigarette passes from cold hand to cold hand and then thrusts hungrily between two lips. Three pairs of eyes watch covetously. One pair watches the leaves in the wind.

The end of the fag burns brightly as he inhales, and his eyes light up to match it. They both dim simultaneously as it's withdrawn from his mouth and passed around the circle. A cloud of shadowy smoke has gathered above the group now, and even those who wait their turn exhale warm clouds into the crisp air, creating a wispy white camouflage. Only their loud hollering and laughing infiltrates the smoke screen. Insults are hurled across the circle, packaged lovingly in a haze of cigarette breath and smoke. Sporting skills are slated; questionable fashions are faulted, and the new kid is teased with rumour-based banter and dubious theories about why he has moved.

The new kid is too busy watching the leaves to even notice; their titter-tatter as they scuff across the floor louder in his ears than anything the other boys are saying. Some swirl up suddenly as they catch an updraft, lifting out of the dank alleyway and over the roofs of the shops. They are free to go anywhere now, he thinks, but how brown and decayed they have to become before they build up the courage to shake free from their branches.

'Emmanuel.' Four voices call in unison. He looks up with

misty eyes and a sea of angry ones stare back. An outstretched arm waves the cigarette in his face.

'Come on Emmanuel, it will burn out if you don't hurry up.' Emmanuel rubs his fingertips together, exposed through his fingerless gloves, and takes the cigarette. He licks his lips in anticipation as he guides the unfamiliar object towards his mouth. Much to the impatience of the others he pauses to adjust his grip, moving his fingers closer to the smouldering glow at the end, so that he could now feel a slight burning sensation pierce his skin. He could touch whatever he wanted here, he thinks.

Emmanuel's fingertips and lips tingle as he follows the other boys down the frosty street. Ahead of him they saunter slowly in their winter jackets and skinny jeans, ignoring the build-up of pedestrian traffic they're causing behind them. Emmanuel attempts a saunter too, although he wears heavy blue jeans which are at least two sizes too big for him, turned up severely at the bottom and held up with a belt at the top. As well as that he has a bulky rainproof jacket thrown over a chequered, long-sleeved shirt. All have been bought from a charity shop by his brother. Everything he is given by his brother is long-sleeved and heavy.

He thinks of his brother waiting back at the flat. His dark, disappointed eyes. His tired, cracked lips, still acclimatising to the cold. Emmanuel had breathed in the cold air gratefully as they stepped off the plane, had enjoyed the prickle of the hairs inside his sleeves, and the clouds drifting across the sun like silk curtains. His brother had shivered.

Heat brought anger, he thinks. Everyone used to be so angry, but here it felt different. The blood runs slower in the cold. His brother will calm eventually, he thinks, and perhaps the cold will change other things too.

The group comes to a standstill as they study the listings

outside the cinema. Emmanuel loiters near them, glancing up at the icicles hanging from the canopy above: long and pointed, perfectly trapped in position and held precariously above him. He begins flicking through the rack of flyers beside him, warming himself on their vivid colours and heated images: a burning building, a generic superhero clad in cartoon-like colours, a half-naked man sweating.

As he riffles through the flyers he thinks of the sun. He thinks of the African sun and the English Sun; so different and yet the same. The African sun is large and unforgiving. An authority in the sky, watching over you constantly. He remembers the sunlight bursting through the shadows and probing at his terrified, pleasure-filled eyes. He remembers the heat on his naked body. He remembers the dozens of tiny suns, like fireballs, reflected in horrified eyes.

A jogger in tight red shorts pounds past the cinema. Emmanuel watches him through the corner of his eye as he continues to finger the flyers. He doesn't hear the other boys arguing about which film to watch.

He thinks of the last time he'd seen that enormous African sun, as his brother hurried him into the airport, and the first time he saw the English sun as he stepped off the plane. The mysterious paleness of it, as if it were a reflection in a lake. The English sun is cool and reserved. It turns a blind eye and lets you breathe in the cold air of possibility. The air is full of movement and wind here too, not thick with motionless dust and heat. Everything is cool here, he thinks, except perhaps the touch of smooth, pink skin.

With a flutter of bright colours the whole rack of flyers suddenly turns over, as a passionately kissing couple tumble into it. The clatter echoes through the chilly evening air of the emptying streets and Emmanuel feels a million eyes fall on him. He freezes, tall and thin, gripping the one leaflet he has been looking at. With a jerk of his exposed fingers he tosses it to the floor quickly, but it skids loudly on the icy pavement and the bronzed body of the half-naked man seems to glow. The blood in his face warms.

On the way home Emmanuel gets a call from his brother saying he is going to make kedjenou for tea and could he pick up some chicken.

Emmanuel goes into a corner shop and picks up a frozen chicken from the deep chest freezer, placing it under his arm. The ice cascades down his coat and leaves it wet.

As he walks along the quiet street with the cold chicken pressed against him, Emmanuel thinks of burning buildings and sweat. He thinks of the hot African sun and warm brown skin. He thinks of cigarettes and slow-cooked kedjenou. All the while he runs his hand across a wire fence, brushing off the ice and letting it shower to the floor. His fingers tingle with a fading sharpness.

NOTES ON CONTRIBUTORS

Natasha Borton is an English-language Welsh writer with an MA Creative Writing at Edge Hill University. She has been published in *Erbacce, For Books Sake* and *The Sublime* and performs regularly around north Wales and the North West. Natasha performs as part of the Voicebox collective, and has worked with Roundhouse London in their international collective Talking Doorsteps. She has performed at the Lowry, the Bluecoat and the Everyman. She currently lives in Wrexham, north Wales.

Ellen Davies is twenty-four and lives in the Rhondda. She has a BA in English Literature and an MA in Creative Writing from Cardiff University. Her debut poetry pamphlet, *Accent,* was published by Cinnamon Press earlier this year.

Mari Ellis Dunning is a Welsh poet and story writer who has recently completed her MA in Creative Writing at Aberystwyth University. As well as having self-published an ebook entitled *Between the Sheets: a Fairy Tale Collection,* Mari's work has featured in several online publications. She also recently co-edited *Wales Within,* an anthology of local creative writing, including poetry and prose, printed by the university and sold in bookshops across Aberystwyth. Her children's picture book about friendship and diversity, *Percy the Pompom Bear* will be published in May 2016 by Rowanvale Books. In addition to writing, Mari likes coffee, heavy eyeliner and dogs.

Chelsea Gilmore is a recent English Literature graduate from Cardiff University. She spent a great deal of her undergraduate degree with the Creative Writing department and writes a mixture of poetry and short stories. If she isn't trying to make readers cry, she is trying to make children laugh as a long-time volunteer of Girl Guiding.

Sam Graydon has recently graduated from the University of Oxford, where he read English Language and Literature. In amongst his studies, he co-edited an arts magazine, organised events for the Oxford University Poetry Society, and had a radio show discussing the origins of different musical genres. He is particularly interested in the Romantics and Victorians and their poetry, and more broadly, in the genre of comedy. He currently works at Tate, surround by art.

Emily Green was born in Devon in 1992, grew up in Carmarthenshire, but has lived in Cardiff since 2008, adopting it as her hometown. She graduated from Cardiff Metropolitan University in 2015 with a degree in English and Creative writing and is currently a Creative Writing MA student at Cardiff University.

Natalie Ann Holborow is an MA graduate in Creative Writing at Swansea University and is currently writer-in-residence at the Dylan Thomas birthplace. By day, she works with words as an Instructional Designer, and by night she is compere of Mad As Birds, a monthly spoken word and music open mic in her lovely, ugly town. She is the winner of the Terry Hetherington Award 2015 and has been highly commended for various others including the Bridport Prize, Hippocrates Prize, Jane Martin Poetry Prize and was longlisted for the National Poetry Prize 2015. She has recently been published in

The Stinging Fly and *The New Welsh Review*. She wants to see her debut poetry collection published, the first draft of her novel written, and to see the Swans move up in the league table by 2017.

Kevin Hudson is from Cardiff. His fiction is currently unpublished, however he has written some articles for online news sites. Originally from a small farm in Shropshire, Kevin now attends Cardiff University, studying English Literature and Journalism. He is twenty-one years old and entering the final year of his degree.

Niall Robert Ivin is a twenty-one-year-old student (soon to be alumni) of Cardiff Metropolitan University studying English and Creative Writing. He was born in Newport and raised in Risca. He is currently in the process of finding employment with an aim to undertake an MA in Creative Writing at Cardiff University in 2016. Alongside this he intends to continue writing short fiction. He hopes that success in the Robin Reeves prize will aid him in beginning to carve a place for himself in the Welsh literary scene.

Ianto Jones is a twenty-one-year-old poet and songwriter from Cardiff who has recently finished studying for a degree in English and Creative writing in Aberystwyth University. Ianto's poetry often deals with overcoming adversity like the loss of somone or something and how to overcome these losses. Ianto's work has been published once before in *The Wait Anthology* (Camrose Media, 2014), which was a fundraising anthology for Cancer Research UK.

Kitty May Howell Jones was born in 1998 in Berkshire, England. Both of her parents are Welsh and they moved to

Wales when she was six. Kitty has just finished her AS levels at Monmouth Comprehensive School, sitting English Literature, English Language and Art. She will stay at MCS to sit her A levels and would like to take English Literature (possibly with Creative Writing) at university. She enjoys writing poetry in and outside of school, and entering writing competitions such as this one and would like to make a career out of writing in the future.

Originally from Llanpumsaint, Carmarthenshire, **Miriam Elin Jones** is currently studying in the Welsh Department at Aberystwyth University. She writes academically during the day, and creatively when she has the time. She has published short stories in *TuChwith* and *Y Ddraig* magazines, and writes in Welsh and English.

Born and raised in the Preseli Mountains, **Erin Mathias** attended *Ysgol y Preseli* before going on to read English at the University of Exeter. She now lives in Cardiff, wears smocks a lot, wishes her eyelashes were longer, and loves tool shops and windy days.

Eve Elizabeth Moriarty writes poetry and fiction. After completing her BA in English at Swansea University, she studied MA Creative Writing at Lancaster, where she compiled and edited *Lightsink*, an anthology of writers from the programme. Her work was commended in the 2013 Terry Hetherington award. Eve now lives in Swansea with her pet rat, where she compères and organises spoken word events, including the popular HOWL Poetry Sessions.

Sam Pryce is an eighteen-year-old aspiring writer and performer from Porthcawl in south Wales. He is also a published theatre critic, writing for *Young Critics, Arts Scene in Wales* and *Wales Online*. He has previously performed two of his short stories at events run by Dirty Protest and Artes Mundi. His favourite writers include Samuel Beckett, Harold Pinter and Martin Amis. Sam is currently studying English at UCL. You can follow him @samofthepryce or read his bookish blog at: stuffsamreads.blogspot.co.uk

Sara Robles recently submitted a novel for an MPhil at the University of South Wales after completing her degree in Creative and Professional Writing at the same university. One of her poems appears in an anthology entitled *Love is in the Air*, published by Forward Poetry.

Durre S. Mughal has an MA in Creative Writing from Cardiff Metropolitan University. She writes fiction, non-fiction and poetry about gender, ethnicity, mental health and urban environments. She has written for *NAWE, The Sprout* and *Wales Arts Review*. She can be found on Twitter at: @Durre_Shahwar.

Nineteen years ago, **Paige Smeaton** was born in Aberystwyth. Up until recently she could say she lived there all her life. Now she is reading English Literature in England but still runs away back home whenever possible. Previously unpublished, Paige has read her stories at poetry readings and done some exhibition work in Aberystwyth where she was a key member of the Ceredigion Heritage Youth Panel. There Paige helped curate, design and write labels for the exhibitions 'Clockwise', 'aMaze' and 'Spectacular Sideshows' at Amgueddfa Ceredigion Museum.

Natalie Thomas was born in Swansea but grew up in the English countryside. She spent her childhood dreaming of becoming a writer and wrote her first short story about a talking pony when she was nine years old. She now studies English Literature at Cardiff University. After finishing her degree, Natalie hopes to complete a Masters in Creative Writing. She is driven by her love for poetry and hopes to one day publish a collection of her work.

JUDGE'S BIO

Rachel Trezise was born in the Rhondda valley in south Wales where she still lives. She studied at Glamorgan and Limerick Universities. Her first novel *In and Out of the Goldfish Bowl* was published by Parthian in 2000. Her first short fiction collection *Fresh Apples* won the Dylan Thomas Prize in 2006. Her second short fiction collection *Cosmic Latte* won the Edge Hill Short Story Prize Readers' Choice Award in 2014. Her first full-length play *Tonypandemonium* was staged by National Theatre Wales in 2013. She also writes non fiction.

JUDGE'S REPORT

Judging the 2015 Robin Reeves Prize for Young Writers has been a rewarding experience for me. Over the past couple of years I've spent a significant amount of my time delivering short story workshops to young people in the South Wales Valleys as part of the Rhys Davies Education and Outreach programme, part of the South Wales Literature Initiative, taking Rhys Davies' work as an inspiration and starting point and engaging young people involved with RCT Young Carers, Valley Kids and Treorchy, Bridgend and Porth County Comprehensive schools in the practice of short story writing. I also recently judged a short story competition for Rhondda secondary schools to mark Rhondda novelist Gwyn Thomas' centenary. Now, as the Rhys Davies Education and Outreach programme draws to a close, what better way to round off my work with young people than by reading the entries to this year's Robin Reeves prize? The theme of this year's competition, 'Out of the Ashes – Overcoming Adversity' is particularly appropriate since it is a theme close to my own heart and work.

Judging writing of any type can never be an uncomplicated task since the intention of all writers are distinctly different. A theme helps a little, but not much, because themes can only be relative to any given participant's experience and outlook. In order to begin to find good writing I always look for a few basic literary ingredients: a hook at the beginning of the work; something compelling enough to grab my hand and drag me in, a clear narrative arc that guides me assuredly from the start to finish and at least one character or narrator who can demonstrate all of the complex implications of human nature so that I, and hopefully everybody else, can recognise themselves reflected therein. After that it's pretty much down to voice. Though literary voice is an inexact science and quite often a matter of taste, a strong and original voice is instantly identifiable. It may not always tell us what we want to hear but it will be saying something that cannot be ignored. Voice is a vital factor in the three pieces of work I chose finally for the runner's-up and winner, bold and unapologetic in *'Fy'n laeth'*, confident and composed in *'Caer Alyn'*. In the winning story 'The Bees', voice thunders out like a force of nature. And while 'voice' may sound like a tremendously basic facet, we must remember how difficult voice is to master as a young writer. Habitually I hear creative writing tutor friends lament the fact their MA students are still waiting to discover 'their voice', and yet here is an anthology full of 17-24-year-old's work categorically bursting with it.

'Fy'n laeth' I chose for its warmth and playfulness in the face of a timely concern: Welsh identity, *'Caer Alyn'* for its arresting, albeit unnerving imagery of an archaeological dig at an Iron Age hillfort. 'The Bees' I chose for its dialogue which struck me as candid and sincere. Although the story doesn't (and does not promise to) tackle any particular issue, it does ably demonstrate the author's skill at capturing a slice of modern Welsh family life.

Rachel Trezise

EDITOR'S BIO

Christina Thatcher is a PhD student and postgraduate tutor at Cardiff University where she studies how creative writing can impact the lives of people bereaved by addiction. Christina keeps busy off campus too by delivering creative writing workshops across south Wales, running projects for organizations like Making Minds and the Welsh Writers' Trust, coordinating literature events for the Made in Roath Festival, and more. Her work has featured in a number of publications including *The London Magazine*, *Planet Magazine*, and the *Lampeter Review*. Her poetry collection, *More than you were*, was recently shortlisted in Bare Fiction's Debut Poetry Collection Competition. To learn more about Christina's work please visit her blog: https://collectingwords.wordpress.com or follow her on Twitter @writetoempower.

WELSH WRITERS' TRUST

Find out more about the Welsh Writers Trust at
https://welshwritertrust.wordpress.com/